but just worry about you,
and what you hold to be true.

a not-walking-pile-of-shit
does what it has got to do.

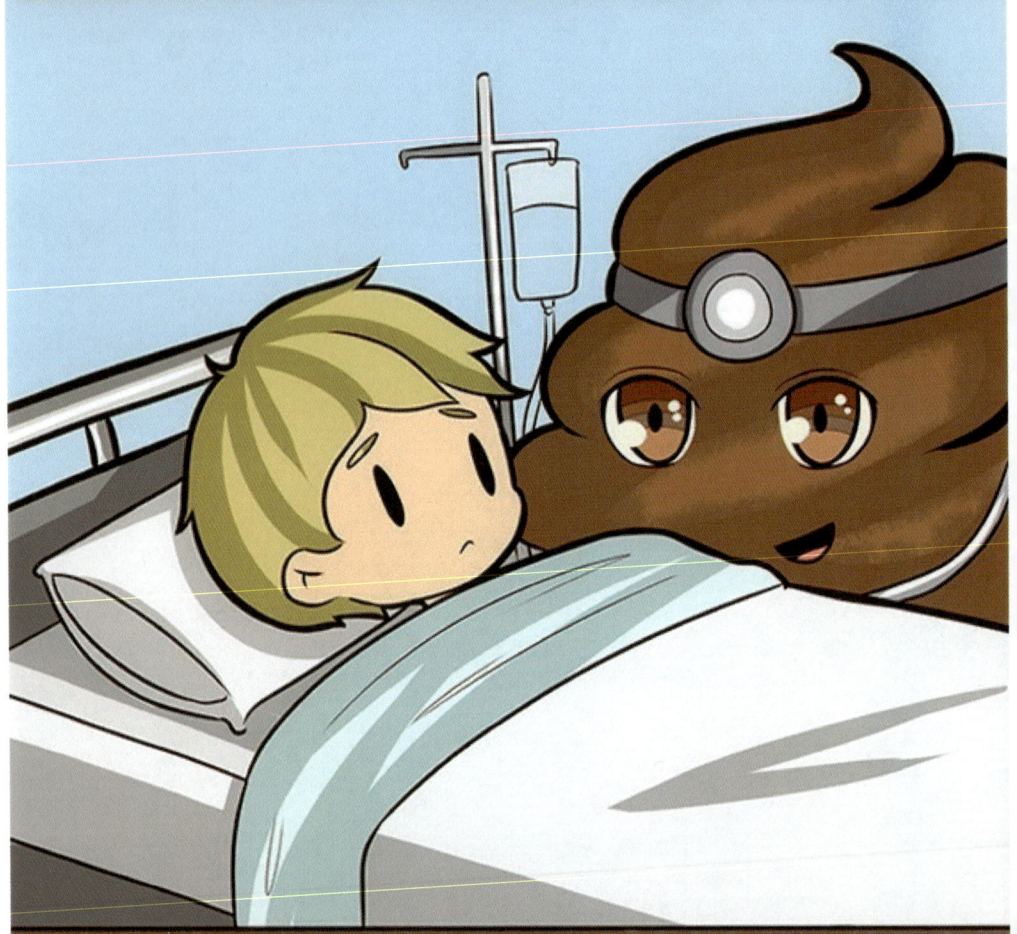

we know school mostly sucks ass, but it is mostly worth it.

it's either a few years shitty or your entire purpose.

a not-walking-pile-of-shit

does what it has got to do.

Relax a little as you get ready for sleep, you have a date tomorrow... but in just a few hours ...you met online, you'll finally meet.

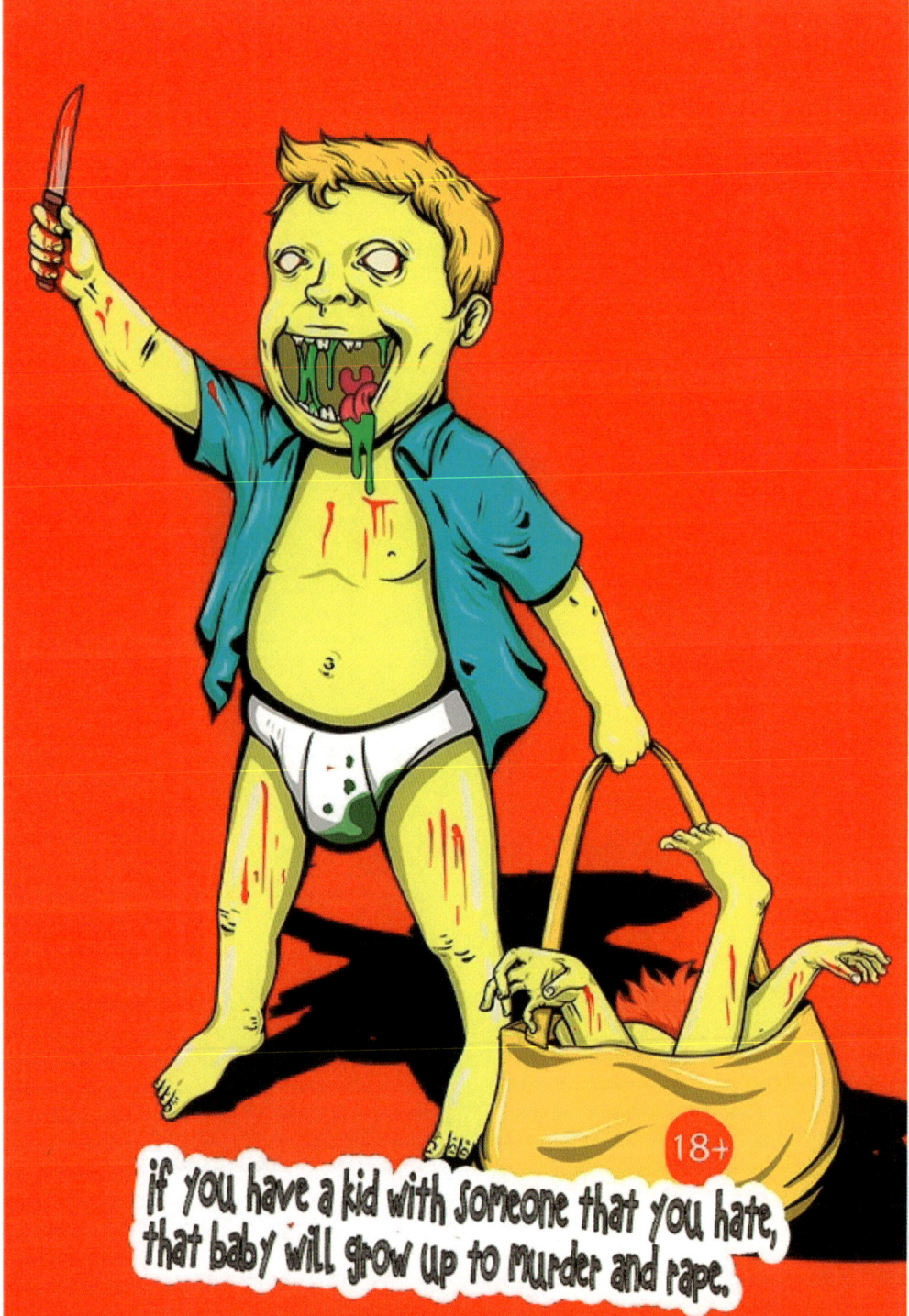

artwork by

Page 1 - Sabhee and Pablo Peruzzi
Page 2 - key dh
Page 3 - Pablo Peruzzi
Page 4 - kevin regan
Page 5 - Pablo Peruzzi
Page 6 - Pablo Peruzzi
Page 7 - Pablo Peruzzi
Page 8 - azurel
Page 9 - jeevazartz
Page 10 - Philip Capili
Page 11 - a besarab
Page 12 - Nikita garets
Page 13 - Lord Cthulhu
Page 14 - yami
Page 15 - gonmuki (andi triyanta)
Page 16 - C.P. Milan
Page 17 - Lilith Valebali
Page 18 - key dh
Page 19 - Neha and Pablo Peruzzi
Page 20 - rosa Paula
Page 21 - alishba khan
Page 22 - alexander krasnyk
Page 23 - Lana Shybinska
Page 24 - abdul qhodir
Page 25 - Elie Nuryanti
Page 26 - jbnusinart
Page 27 - Lule Quiroz
Page 28 - bunnyonthemoon
Page 29 - j.b. qadri
Page 30 - kevin regan
Page 31 - jbnusinart
Page 32 - Small Jyoti
Page 33 - Paolo Savelli
Page 34 - Mouahd
Page 35 - Philip Capili
Page 36 - kevin regan
Page 37 - wandering artist
Page 38 - a besarab
Page 39 - Elie Nuryanti
Page 40 - Small Jyoti
Page 41 - Cain
font - khryskreations
Cover - krrjuuus

how to not be a walking pile of shit by darrin andrews
Published by createspace
4900 LaCross road
North Charleston, SC 29406
www.createspace.com
© 2017

all rights reserved. No portion of this book may be reproduced in any form without permission from the publisher, except as permitted by U.S. copyright law.
for permissions contact:
mondocoolvideos@gmail.com
ISBN-13: 978-1979640770
ISBN-10: 1979640777

and because i'll probably never have this chance again, i want to thank:

joe for being a great friend/roommate and putting up with my shit, most my amazing co-workers, but especially fran-fran for having an inspiring, beautiful soul and sam for having the best work ethic ever witnessed in any human being. also, i guess my friends, family, and the folks that raised me are okay, too.

and i should thank all the piles of shit that inspired this book, but fuck those guys.

... including Chris.

fuck you, Chris.

also, special thanks to bacons stanford.

Proof

Made in the USA
Columbia, SC
29 November 2017